I0499922

Job Title

Contact Information

Address

Date

Permit Number

Invoice Number

Materials

Mileage

Hours

Job Details

Payment Received

Costs

Payment Method

Job Title

Contact Information

Date

Address

Permit Number   Invoice Number

Materials

Mileage

Hours

Job Details

Payment Received

Payment Method

Costs

Job Title

Contact Information

Date

Address

Permit Number

Invoice Number

Materials

Mileage

Hours

Job Details

Payment Received

Payment Method

Costs

Job Title

Contact Information

Date

Address

Permit Number

Invoice Number

Materials

Mileage

Hours

Job Details

Payment Received

Payment Method

Costs

Job Title

Contact Information

Address

Date

Permit Number

Invoice Number

Materials

Mileage

Hours

Job Details

Payment Received

Costs

Payment Method

Job Title

Contact Information

Date

Address

Permit Number

Invoice Number

Materials

Mileage

Hours

Job Details

Payment Received

Payment Method

Costs

Job Title

Contact Information

Date

Address

Permit Number   Invoice Number

Materials

Mileage

Hours

Job Details

Payment Received

Payment Method

Costs

Job Title

Contact Information

Date

Address

Permit Number

Invoice Number

Materials

Mileage

Hours

Job Details

Payment Received

Payment Method

Costs

Job Title

Contact Information

Address

Date

Permit Number

Invoice Number

Materials

Mileage

Hours

Job Details

Payment Received

Costs

Payment Method

Job Title

Contact Information

Date

Address

Permit Number

Invoice Number

Materials

Mileage

Hours

Job Details

Payment Received

Payment Method

Costs

Job Title

Contact Information

Address

Date

Permit Number

Invoice Number

Materials

Mileage

Hours

Job Details

Payment Received

Costs

Payment Method

Job Title

Contact Information

Date

Address

Permit Number

Invoice Number

Materials

Mileage

Hours

Job Details

Payment Received

Payment Method

Costs

Job Title

Contact Information

Date

Address

Permit Number

Invoice Number

Materials

Mileage

Hours

Job Details

Payment Received

Payment Method

Costs

Job Title

Contact Information

Date

Address

Permit Number

Invoice Number

Materials

Mileage

Hours

Job Details

Payment Received

Payment Method

Costs

Job Title

Contact Information

Date

Address

Permit Number

Invoice Number

Materials

Mileage

Hours

Job Details

Payment Received

Payment Method

Costs

Job Title	Address
Contact Information	
Date	Permit Number Invoice Number

Materials	Mileage
	Hours

Job Details

Payment Received	Costs
Payment Method	

Job Title

Contact Information

Date

Address

Permit Number

Invoice Number

Materials

Mileage

Hours

Job Details

Payment Received

Payment Method

Costs

Job Title

Contact Information

Date

Address

Permit Number

Invoice Number

Materials

Mileage

Hours

Job Details

Payment Received

Costs

Payment Method

Job Title

Contact Information

Date

Address

Permit Number

Invoice Number

Materials

Mileage

Hours

Job Details

Payment Received

Costs

Payment Method

Job Title

Contact Information

Date

Address

Permit Number

Invoice Number

Materials

Mileage

Hours

Job Details

Payment Received

Payment Method

Costs

Job Title

Contact Information

Date

Address

Permit Number

Invoice Number

Materials

Mileage

Hours

Job Details

Payment Received

Payment Method

Costs

Job Title

Contact Information

Date

Address

Permit Number

Invoice Number

Materials

Mileage

Hours

Job Details

Payment Received

Payment Method

Costs

Job Title

Contact Information

Address

Date

Permit Number

Invoice Number

Materials

Mileage

Hours

Job Details

Payment Received

Costs

Payment Method

Job Title

Contact Information

Date

Address

Permit Number

Invoice Number

Materials

Mileage

Hours

Job Details

Payment Received

Payment Method

Costs

Job Title

Contact Information

Date

Address

Permit Number

Invoice Number

Materials

Mileage

Hours

Job Details

Payment Received

Payment Method

Costs

Job Title

Contact Information

Date

Address

Permit Number

Invoice Number

Materials

Mileage

Hours

Job Details

Payment Received

Payment Method

Costs

Job Title

Contact Information

Address

Date

Permit Number

Invoice Number

Materials

Mileage

Hours

Job Details

Payment Received

Costs

Payment Method

Job Title	Address
Contact Information	
Date	Permit Number Invoice Number

Materials	Mileage
	Hours

Job Details

Payment Received	Costs
Payment Method	

Job Title

Contact Information

Date

Address

Permit Number   Invoice Number

Materials

Mileage

Hours

Job Details

Payment Received

Payment Method

Costs

Job Title

Contact Information

Date

Address

Permit Number   Invoice Number

Materials

Mileage

Hours

Job Details

Payment Received

Payment Method

Costs

Job Title

Contact Information

Date

Address

Permit Number

Invoice Number

Materials

Mileage

Hours

Job Details

Payment Received

Payment Method

Costs

Job Title

Contact Information

Date

Address

Permit Number

Invoice Number

Materials

Mileage

Hours

Job Details

Payment Received

Payment Method

Costs

Job Title

Contact Information

Date

Address

Permit Number

Invoice Number

Materials

Mileage

Hours

Job Details

Payment Received

Payment Method

Costs

Job Title

Contact Information

Date

Address

Permit Number

Invoice Number

Materials

Mileage

Hours

Job Details

Payment Received

Payment Method

Costs

Job Title

Contact Information

Address

Date

Permit Number

Invoice Number

Materials

Mileage

Hours

Job Details

Payment Received

Costs

Payment Method

Job Title

Contact Information

Date

Address

Permit Number

Invoice Number

Materials

Mileage

Hours

Job Details

Payment Received

Payment Method

Costs

Job Title

Contact Information

Date

Address

Permit Number   Invoice Number

Materials

Mileage

Hours

Job Details

Payment Received

Payment Method

Costs

Job Title

Contact Information

Date

Address

Permit Number

Invoice Number

Materials

Mileage

Hours

Job Details

Payment Received

Payment Method

Costs

Job Title

Contact Information

Date

Address

Permit Number

Invoice Number

Materials

Mileage

Hours

Job Details

Payment Received

Costs

Payment Method

Job Title	Address
Contact Information	
Date	Permit Number Invoice Number

Materials	Mileage
	Hours

Job Details

Payment Received	Costs
Payment Method	

Job Title

Contact Information

Date

Address

Permit Number   Invoice Number

Materials

Mileage

Hours

Job Details

Payment Received

Payment Method

Costs

Job Title

Contact Information

Date

Address

Permit Number

Invoice Number

Materials

Mileage

Hours

Job Details

Payment Received

Costs

Payment Method

Job Title

Contact Information

Date

Address

Permit Number

Invoice Number

Materials

Mileage

Hours

Job Details

Payment Received

Costs

Payment Method

Job Title

Contact Information

Date

Address

Permit Number

Invoice Number

Materials

Mileage

Hours

Job Details

Payment Received

Payment Method

Costs

Job Title

Contact Information

Date

Address

Permit Number

Invoice Number

Materials

Mileage

Hours

Job Details

Payment Received

Payment Method

Costs

Job Title

Contact Information

Date

Address

Permit Number

Invoice Number

Materials

Mileage

Hours

Job Details

Payment Received

Payment Method

Costs

Job Title

Contact Information

Address

Date

Permit Number

Invoice Number

Materials

Mileage

Hours

Job Details

Payment Received

Costs

Payment Method

Job Title

Contact Information

Date

Address

Permit Number

Invoice Number

Materials

Mileage

Hours

Job Details

Payment Received

Payment Method

Costs

Job Title

Address

Contact Information

Date

Permit Number

Invoice Number

Materials

Mileage

Hours

Job Details

Payment Received

Costs

Payment Method

Job Title

Contact Information

Date

Address

Permit Number

Invoice Number

Materials

Mileage

Hours

Job Details

Payment Received

Payment Method

Costs

Job Title

Contact Information

Date

Address

Permit Number

Invoice Number

Materials

Mileage

Hours

Job Details

Payment Received

Payment Method

Costs

Job Title

Contact Information

Date

Address

Permit Number   Invoice Number

Materials

Mileage

Hours

Job Details

Payment Received

Payment Method

Costs

Job Title

Contact Information

Date

Address

Permit Number

Invoice Number

Materials

Mileage

Hours

Job Details

Payment Received

Costs

Payment Method

Job Title

Contact Information

Date

Address

Permit Number

Invoice Number

Materials

Mileage

Hours

Job Details

Payment Received

Costs

Payment Method

Job Title

Contact Information

Date

Address

Permit Number

Invoice Number

Materials

Mileage

Hours

Job Details

Payment Received

Payment Method

Costs

Job Title

Contact Information

Date

Address

Permit Number

Invoice Number

Materials

Mileage

Hours

Job Details

Payment Received

Payment Method

Costs

Job Title

Contact Information

Date

Address

Permit Number

Invoice Number

Materials

Mileage

Hours

Job Details

Payment Received

Payment Method

Costs

Job Title

Contact Information

Date

Address

Permit Number

Invoice Number

Materials

Mileage

Hours

Job Details

Payment Received

Payment Method

Costs

Job Title

Contact Information

Address

Date

Permit Number

Invoice Number

Materials

Mileage

Hours

Job Details

Payment Received

Costs

Payment Method

Job Title

Contact Information

Date

Address

Permit Number

Invoice Number

Materials

Mileage

Hours

Job Details

Payment Received

Payment Method

Costs

Job Title

Contact Information

Date

Address

Permit Number

Invoice Number

Materials

Mileage

Hours

Job Details

Payment Received

Payment Method

Costs

Job Title	Address	
Contact Information		
Date	Permit Number	Invoice Number

Materials	Mileage
	Hours

Job Details

Payment Received	Costs
Payment Method	

Job Title

Contact Information

Date

Address

Permit Number

Invoice Number

Materials

Mileage

Hours

Job Details

Payment Received

Payment Method

Costs

Job Title

Contact Information

Date

Address

Permit Number

Invoice Number

Materials

Mileage

Hours

Job Details

Payment Received

Payment Method

Costs

Job Title

Contact Information

Date

Address

Permit Number

Invoice Number

Materials

Mileage

Hours

Job Details

Payment Received

Costs

Payment Method

Job Title

Contact Information

Date

Address

Permit Number

Invoice Number

Materials

Mileage

Hours

Job Details

Payment Received

Payment Method

Costs

Job Title

Contact Information

Date

Address

Permit Number

Invoice Number

Materials

Mileage

Hours

Job Details

Payment Received

Payment Method

Costs

Job Title

Contact Information

Date

Address

Permit Number

Invoice Number

Materials

Mileage

Hours

Job Details

Payment Received

Payment Method

Costs

Job Title

Contact Information

Date

Address

Permit Number

Invoice Number

Materials

Mileage

Hours

Job Details

Payment Received

Costs

Payment Method

Job Title

Contact Information

Date

Address

Permit Number

Invoice Number

Materials

Mileage

Hours

Job Details

Payment Received

Costs

Payment Method

Job Title

Address

Contact Information

Date

Permit Number

Invoice Number

Materials

Mileage

Hours

Job Details

Payment Received

Costs

Payment Method

Job Title

Contact Information

Date

Address

Permit Number

Invoice Number

Materials

Mileage

Hours

Job Details

Payment Received

Payment Method

Costs

Job Title

Contact Information

Date

Address

Permit Number

Invoice Number

Materials

Mileage

Hours

Job Details

Payment Received

Payment Method

Costs

Job Title

Contact Information

Date

Address

Permit Number

Invoice Number

Materials

Mileage

Hours

Job Details

Payment Received

Costs

Payment Method

Job Title

Contact Information

Address

Date

Permit Number

Invoice Number

Materials

Mileage

Hours

Job Details

Payment Received

Costs

Payment Method

Job Title

Contact Information

Date

Address

Permit Number

Invoice Number

Materials

Mileage

Hours

Job Details

Payment Received

Payment Method

Costs

Job Title

Contact Information

Address

Date

Permit Number

Invoice Number

Materials

Mileage

Hours

Job Details

Payment Received

Costs

Payment Method

Job Title	Address	
Contact Information		
Date	Permit Number	Invoice Number

Materials	Mileage
	Hours

Job Details

Payment Received	Costs
Payment Method	

Job Title

Contact Information

Date

Address

Permit Number

Invoice Number

Materials

Mileage

Hours

Job Details

Payment Received

Costs

Payment Method

Job Title

Contact Information

Date

Address

Permit Number

Invoice Number

Materials

Mileage

Hours

Job Details

Payment Received

Costs

Payment Method

Job Title

Contact Information

Date

Address

Permit Number

Invoice Number

Materials

Mileage

Hours

Job Details

Payment Received

Payment Method

Costs

Job Title

Contact Information

Address

Date

Permit Number

Invoice Number

Materials

Mileage

Hours

Job Details

Payment Received

Costs

Payment Method

Job Title

Contact Information

Date

Address

Permit Number   Invoice Number

Materials

Mileage

Hours

Job Details

Payment Received

Payment Method

Costs

Job Title	Address	
Contact Information		
Date	Permit Number	Invoice Number

Materials	Mileage
	Hours

Job Details

Payment Received	Costs
Payment Method	

Job Title

Contact Information

Date

Address

Permit Number

Invoice Number

Materials

Mileage

Hours

Job Details

Payment Received

Payment Method

Costs

Job Title

Contact Information

Date

Address

Permit Number

Invoice Number

Materials

Mileage

Hours

Job Details

Payment Received

Payment Method

Costs

Job Title

Contact Information

Address

Date

Permit Number

Invoice Number

Materials

Mileage

Hours

Job Details

Payment Received

Costs

Payment Method

Job Title

Contact Information

Date

Address

Permit Number   Invoice Number

Materials

Mileage

Hours

Job Details

Payment Received   Costs

Payment Method

Job Title

Contact Information

Address

Date

Permit Number

Invoice Number

Materials

Mileage

Hours

Job Details

Payment Received

Costs

Payment Method

Job Title

Contact Information

Date

Address

Permit Number

Invoice Number

Materials

Mileage

Hours

Job Details

Payment Received

Costs

Payment Method

Job Title

Contact Information

Date

Address

Permit Number

Invoice Number

Materials

Mileage

Hours

Job Details

Payment Received

Payment Method

Costs

Job Title

Contact Information

Date

Address

Permit Number

Invoice Number

Materials

Mileage

Hours

Job Details

Payment Received

Payment Method

Costs

Job Title

Contact Information

Address

Date

Permit Number

Invoice Number

Materials

Mileage

Hours

Job Details

Payment Received

Costs

Payment Method

Job Title

Contact Information

Date

Address

Permit Number

Invoice Number

Materials

Mileage

Hours

Job Details

Payment Received

Payment Method

Costs

Job Title	Address	
Contact Information		
Date	Permit Number	Invoice Number

Materials	Mileage
	Hours

Job Details

Payment Received	Costs
Payment Method	

Job Title

Contact Information

Date

Address

Permit Number

Invoice Number

Materials

Mileage

Hours

Job Details

Payment Received

Payment Method

Costs

Job Title

Contact Information

Date

Address

Permit Number

Invoice Number

Materials

Mileage

Hours

Job Details

Payment Received

Payment Method

Costs

Job Title

Contact Information

Date

Address

Permit Number   Invoice Number

Materials

Mileage

Hours

Job Details

Payment Received

Payment Method

Costs

Job Title

Contact Information

Address

Date

Permit Number

Invoice Number

Materials

Mileage

Hours

Job Details

Payment Received

Costs

Payment Method

Job Title

Contact Information

Date

Address

Permit Number

Invoice Number

Materials

Mileage

Hours

Job Details

Payment Received

Payment Method

Costs

Job Title

Contact Information

Date

Address

Permit Number

Invoice Number

Materials

Mileage

Hours

Job Details

Payment Received

Payment Method

Costs

Job Title

Contact Information

Date

Address

Permit Number

Invoice Number

Materials

Mileage

Hours

Job Details

Payment Received

Payment Method

Costs

Job Title

Contact Information

Date

Address

Permit Number   Invoice Number

Materials

Mileage

Hours

Job Details

Payment Received

Payment Method

Costs

Job Title

Contact Information

Date

Address

Permit Number

Invoice Number

Materials

Mileage

Hours

Job Details

Payment Received

Payment Method

Costs

Job Title

Contact Information

Address

Date

Permit Number

Invoice Number

Materials

Mileage

Hours

Job Details

Payment Received

Costs

Payment Method

Job Title

Contact Information

Date

Address

Permit Number

Invoice Number

Materials

Mileage

Hours

Job Details

Payment Received

Payment Method

Costs

Job Title

Contact Information

Date

Address

Permit Number

Invoice Number

Materials

Mileage

Hours

Job Details

Payment Received

Payment Method

Costs

Job Title	Address
Contact Information	
Date	Permit Number Invoice Number

Materials	Mileage
	Hours

Job Details

Payment Received	Costs
Payment Method	

Job Title

Contact Information

Date

Address

Permit Number

Invoice Number

Materials

Mileage

Hours

Job Details

Payment Received

Payment Method

Costs

Job Title

Contact Information

Date

Address

Permit Number

Invoice Number

Materials

Mileage

Hours

Job Details

Payment Received

Payment Method

Costs

Job Title

Contact Information

Address

Date

Permit Number

Invoice Number

Materials

Mileage

Hours

Job Details

Payment Received

Payment Method

Costs

Job Title

Contact Information

Date

Address

Permit Number

Invoice Number

Materials

Mileage

Hours

Job Details

Payment Received

Costs

Payment Method

Job Title

Contact Information

Date

Address

Permit Number

Invoice Number

Materials

Mileage

Hours

Job Details

Payment Received

Payment Method

Costs

Job Title

Contact Information

Date

Address

Permit Number

Invoice Number

Materials

Mileage

Hours

Job Details

Payment Received

Payment Method

Costs

Job Title

Contact Information

Date

Address

Permit Number

Invoice Number

Materials

Mileage

Hours

Job Details

Payment Received

Payment Method

Costs

Job Title

Contact Information

Date

Address

Permit Number   Invoice Number

Materials

Mileage

Hours

Job Details

Payment Received

Payment Method

Costs

Job Title

Contact Information

Date

Address

Permit Number

Invoice Number

Materials

Mileage

Hours

Job Details

Payment Received

Costs

Payment Method

Job Title

Contact Information

Date

Address

Permit Number

Invoice Number

Materials

Mileage

Hours

Job Details

Payment Received

Payment Method

Costs

Job Title

Contact Information

Date

Address

Permit Number

Invoice Number

Materials

Mileage

Hours

Job Details

Payment Received

Costs

Payment Method

Job Title

Contact Information

Date

Address

Permit Number

Invoice Number

Materials

Mileage

Hours

Job Details

Payment Received

Payment Method

Costs

Job Title

Contact Information

Date

Address

Permit Number

Invoice Number

Materials

Mileage

Hours

Job Details

Payment Received

Payment Method

Costs

Job Title

Contact Information

Date

Address

Permit Number   Invoice Number

Materials

Mileage

Hours

Job Details

Payment Received

Payment Method

Costs

Job Title

Contact Information

Date

Address

Permit Number

Invoice Number

Materials

Mileage

Hours

Job Details

Payment Received

Payment Method

Costs

Job Title

Contact Information

Date

Address

Permit Number

Invoice Number

Materials

Mileage

Hours

Job Details

Payment Received

Payment Method

Costs

Job Title

Contact Information

Address

Date

Permit Number

Invoice Number

Materials

Mileage

Hours

Job Details

Payment Received

Costs

Payment Method

Job Title

Contact Information

Date

Address

Permit Number

Invoice Number

Materials

Mileage

Hours

Job Details

Payment Received

Costs

Payment Method

Job Title

Contact Information

Address

Date

Permit Number

Invoice Number

Materials

Mileage

Hours

Job Details

Payment Received

Costs

Payment Method

Job Title

Contact Information

Date

Address

Permit Number   Invoice Number

Materials

Mileage

Hours

Job Details

Payment Received   Costs

Payment Method

Job Title

Contact Information

Date

Address

Permit Number

Invoice Number

Materials

Mileage

Hours

Job Details

Payment Received

Costs

Payment Method

Job Title

Contact Information

Date

Address

Permit Number

Invoice Number

Materials

Mileage

Hours

Job Details

Payment Received

Payment Method

Costs

Job Title

Contact Information

Address

Date

Permit Number

Invoice Number

Materials

Mileage

Hours

Job Details

Payment Received

Costs

Payment Method

Job Title

Contact Information

Date

Address

Permit Number

Invoice Number

Materials

Mileage

Hours

Job Details

Payment Received

Payment Method

Costs

Job Title

Contact Information

Date

Address

Permit Number

Invoice Number

Materials

Mileage

Hours

Job Details

Payment Received

Payment Method

Costs

Job Title

Contact Information

Date

Address

Permit Number

Invoice Number

Materials

Mileage

Hours

Job Details

Payment Received

Payment Method

Costs

Job Title

Contact Information

Date

Address

Permit Number

Invoice Number

Materials

Mileage

Hours

Job Details

Payment Received

Payment Method

Costs

Job Title

Contact Information

Address

Date

Permit Number

Invoice Number

Materials

Mileage

Hours

Job Details

Payment Received

Costs

Payment Method

Job Title

Contact Information

Address

Date

Permit Number

Invoice Number

Materials

Mileage

Hours

Job Details

Payment Received

Costs

Payment Method

Job Title

Contact Information

Date

Address

Permit Number

Invoice Number

Materials

Mileage

Hours

Job Details

Payment Received

Payment Method

Costs

Job Title

Contact Information

Date

Address

Permit Number

Invoice Number

Materials

Mileage

Hours

Job Details

Payment Received

Payment Method

Costs

Job Title

Contact Information

Date

Address

Permit Number

Invoice Number

Materials

Mileage

Hours

Job Details

Payment Received

Payment Method

Costs

Job Title

Address

Contact Information

Date

Permit Number

Invoice Number

Materials

Mileage

Hours

Job Details

Payment Received

Costs

Payment Method

Job Title

Contact Information

Date

Address

Permit Number

Invoice Number

Materials

Mileage

Hours

Job Details

Payment Received

Payment Method

Costs

Job Title

Contact Information

Date

Address

Permit Number

Invoice Number

Materials

Mileage

Hours

Job Details

Payment Received

Payment Method

Costs

Job Title

Contact Information

Date

Address

Permit Number

Invoice Number

Materials

Mileage

Hours

Job Details

Payment Received

Payment Method

Costs

Job Title

Contact Information

Date

Address

Permit Number

Invoice Number

Materials

Mileage

Hours

Job Details

Payment Received

Costs

Payment Method

Job Title

Contact Information

Date

Address

Permit Number

Invoice Number

Materials

Mileage

Hours

Job Details

Payment Received

Payment Method

Costs

Job Title

Contact Information

Address

Date

Permit Number

Invoice Number

Materials

Mileage

Hours

Job Details

Payment Received

Costs

Payment Method

Job Title

Contact Information

Date

Address

Permit Number

Invoice Number

Materials

Mileage

Hours

Job Details

Payment Received

Payment Method

Costs

Job Title

Contact Information

Date

Address

Permit Number

Invoice Number

Materials

Mileage

Hours

Job Details

Payment Received

Costs

Payment Method

Job Title

Contact Information

Date

Address

Permit Number

Invoice Number

Materials

Mileage

Hours

Job Details

Payment Received

Payment Method

Costs

Job Title

Contact Information

Date

Address

Permit Number

Invoice Number

Materials

Mileage

Hours

Job Details

Payment Received

Payment Method

Costs

Job Title

Address

Contact Information

Date

Permit Number

Invoice Number

Materials

Mileage

Hours

Job Details

Payment Received

Costs

Payment Method

Job Title

Contact Information

Date

Address

Permit Number

Invoice Number

Materials

Mileage

Hours

Job Details

Payment Received

Costs

Payment Method

Job Title

Contact Information

Date

Address

Permit Number   Invoice Number

Materials

Mileage

Hours

Job Details

Payment Received

Payment Method

Costs

Job Title

Contact Information

Date

Address

Permit Number

Invoice Number

Materials

Mileage

Hours

Job Details

Payment Received

Payment Method

Costs

Job Title	Address
Contact Information	
Date	Permit Number	Invoice Number

Materials	Mileage
	Hours

Job Details

Payment Received	Costs
Payment Method	

Job Title

Contact Information

Date

Address

Permit Number

Invoice Number

Materials

Mileage

Hours

Job Details

Payment Received

Costs

Payment Method

Job Title	Address
Contact Information	
Date	Permit Number Invoice Number

Materials	Mileage
	Hours

Job Details

Payment Received	Costs
Payment Method	

Job Title

Contact Information

Address

Date

Permit Number

Invoice Number

Materials

Mileage

Hours

Job Details

Payment Received

Costs

Payment Method

Job Title

Contact Information

Date

Address

Permit Number

Invoice Number

Materials

Mileage

Hours

Job Details

Payment Received

Payment Method

Costs

Job Title

Contact Information

Date

Address

Permit Number

Invoice Number

Materials

Mileage

Hours

Job Details

Payment Received

Payment Method

Costs

Job Title

Contact Information

Date

Address

Permit Number

Invoice Number

Materials

Mileage

Hours

Job Details

Payment Received

Payment Method

Costs

Job Title

Contact Information

Date

Address

Permit Number

Invoice Number

Materials

Mileage

Hours

Job Details

Payment Received

Payment Method

Costs

Job Title

Contact Information

Date

Address

Permit Number   Invoice Number

Materials

Mileage

Hours

Job Details

Payment Received

Payment Method

Costs

Job Title

Contact Information

Address

Date

Permit Number

Invoice Number

Materials

Mileage

Hours

Job Details

Payment Received

Costs

Payment Method

Job Title

Address

Contact Information

Date

Permit Number

Invoice Number

Materials

Mileage

Hours

Job Details

Payment Received

Costs

Payment Method

Job Title

Contact Information

Address

Date

Permit Number

Invoice Number

Materials

Mileage

Hours

Job Details

Payment Received

Costs

Payment Method

Job Title

Contact Information

Date

Address

Permit Number

Invoice Number

Materials

Mileage

Hours

Job Details

Payment Received

Payment Method

Costs

Job Title

Contact Information

Date

Address

Permit Number

Invoice Number

Materials

Mileage

Hours

Job Details

Payment Received

Payment Method

Costs

Job Title

Contact Information

Date

Address

Permit Number

Invoice Number

Materials

Mileage

Hours

Job Details

Payment Received

Payment Method

Costs

Job Title

Contact Information

Date

Address

Permit Number   Invoice Number

Materials

Mileage

Hours

Job Details

Payment Received

Payment Method

Costs

Job Title

Contact Information

Date

Address

Permit Number

Invoice Number

Materials

Mileage

Hours

Job Details

Payment Received

Payment Method

Costs

Job Title

Contact Information

Date

Address

Permit Number

Invoice Number

Materials

Mileage

Hours

Job Details

Payment Received

Payment Method

Costs

Job Title

Contact Information

Date

Address

Permit Number

Invoice Number

Materials

Mileage

Hours

Job Details

Payment Received

Payment Method

Costs

Job Title

Contact Information

Date

Address

Permit Number

Invoice Number

Materials

Mileage

Hours

Job Details

Payment Received

Payment Method

Costs

Job Title

Contact Information

Date

Address

Permit Number

Invoice Number

Materials

Mileage

Hours

Job Details

Payment Received

Payment Method

Costs

Job Title

Contact Information

Date

Address

Permit Number   Invoice Number

Materials

Mileage

Hours

Job Details

Payment Received

Payment Method

Costs

Job Title

Contact Information

Date

Address

Permit Number   Invoice Number

Materials

Mileage

Hours

Job Details

Payment Received

Payment Method

Costs

Job Title

Contact Information

Date

Address

Permit Number

Invoice Number

Materials

Mileage

Hours

Job Details

Payment Received

Costs

Payment Method

Job Title	Address	
Contact Information		
Date	Permit Number	Invoice Number

Materials	Mileage
	Hours

Job Details

Payment Received	Costs
Payment Method